FUN WITH
PAPER

· HEATHER AMERY ·

NOTE TO PARENTS

Some projects use sharp scissors or an X-Acto knife for cutting paper and cardboard. Adult supervision is necessary. Your children may want to use a piece of thick cardboard as a cutting board. Remind them to press downward when using an X-Acto knife.

A few projects also involve the use of water-based varnish. Talk to your children about appropriate safety measures to take when handling varnish or other potentially hazardous materials. Please note which projects will require your supervision.

ACKNOWLEDGMENTS

Paper models made by Karen Radford,
Brian Robertson, and Anne Sharples
Photographs by David Johnson
Illustrations by Joanna Venus

HAMLYN CHILDREN'S BOOKS
Series Editor : Anne Civardi
Series Designer : Anne Sharples
Production Controller : Linda Spillane

First American edition, 1994

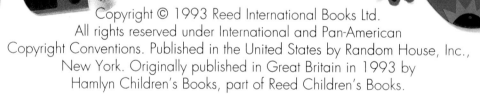

Library of Congress Cataloging-in-Publication Data
Amery, Heather.
Fun with paper / Heather Amery. — 1st American ed.
p.   cm. — (Creative crafts)
Summary: Includes instructions for making a variety of items with
paper, such as flowers, pop-up cards, hats, and masks.
ISBN 0-679-83493-1 (pbk.) — ISBN 0-679-93493-6 (lib. bdg)
1. Paper work — Juvenile literature. [1. Paper work.
2. Handicraft.]   I. Title. II. Series: Creative crafts (New York, N.Y.)
TT870.A46 1994
745.54—dc20   92—51071

Manufactured in Italy
10 9 8 7 6 5 4 3 2 1

CONTENTS

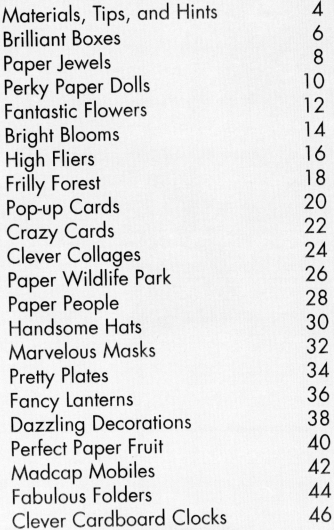

MATERIALS, TIPS, AND HINTS

In this book there are lots of fantastic things for you to make with paper and cardboard. It is a good idea to keep a big cardboard box of useful things, such as toilet paper rolls, paper towel rolls, tinfoil rolls, wrapping paper, empty chocolate boxes, cereal boxes, cardboard boxes, and scraps of wallpaper and tissue paper. Then you will have the things you need when you want to make something.

Collect magazines, catalogs, and travel brochures with color pictures. Cut out pictures of flowers, trees, scenes or anything you like that might be nice to decorate cards or boxes.

Pieces of gold and silver foil from candy wrappers may be useful.

You can buy sheets of construction paper, tissue paper, crepe paper, and posterboard in bright colors.

Collect thin and thick cardboard from old calendars, thick envelopes, and junk mail.

Scissors

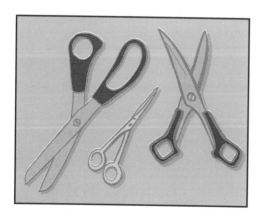

You will need scissors for cutting paper. You will need sharp, pointed ones to make holes in paper and cardboard. For cutting very small or delicate things, use small scissors.

X-Acto knife

Ask an adult to help if you use an X-Acto knife for cutting paper or cardboard. Always use a piece of cardboard as a cutting board, and press downward.

Paints and crayons

Poster, tempera, and watercolor paints, felt-tip pens, and crayons are all useful for decorating things and for writing messages on cards or posters.

4

String and tape

If you only have white string, you can color it with watered-down paint. Let it dry on a sheet of newspaper. You can use double-stick tape instead of glue.

Glue

Buy a jar of children's paste. It is easy to use and has a brush. You can also buy glue with a thin tube at the top so you can squeeze a little out at a time. It is less messy.

HANDY HINTS

Making things can be messy. Before you start, put sheets of old newspaper on the top of the table or floor. And remember to clean up when you have finished. Pick up all the bits of paper that are sticky with glue.

Remember to put the tops and lids back on glue containers, paints, and felt-tip pens so that these materials don't dry out. Wash any glue off your fingers. Otherwise they will get dirty and leave finger marks everywhere.

Keep a ruler handy for measuring things and for drawing and cutting straight lines.

BRILLIANT BOXES

Boxes and baskets are great for keeping all sorts of things in and for packing up presents. These are made out of posterboard and covered with colored paper or decorated with paint. You can make them any size, from very shallow to quite deep, with lids for the boxes.

Decorate the boxes with stars, paper bows, or a pretty border.

Things you need

Posterboard or cardboard
Colored paper
Pencil and ruler
Watercolor or poster paints
Scissors
Tape and strong glue

Shallow box

1. Hold a ruler down on one side of the posterboard, 12 in. x 8 in. Run scissors along the ruler's other edge to make a groove. Do this to all four sides.

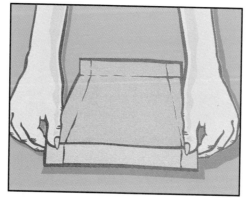

2. Carefully fold up one side of the posterboard along the line of the groove, like this. Unfold it and then carefully fold up the other three sides, one at a time.

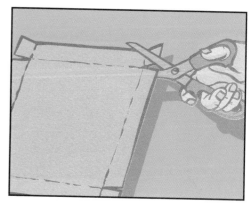

3. Unfold the piece of posterboard and cut along the groove at each corner, as shown. Stop when you reach the groove going the other way.

Paint patterns or flowers, or stick paper shapes on your baskets.

Fold colored paper around a box. Make a cut at each corner. Tuck in the tabs and glue the paper to the box.

HANDY HINTS

You need two sheets of posterboard for each box. Make sure they are the same size before you start.

For a square box, you need square pieces of posterboard, and long pieces of posterboard for long boxes.

To make a deep box, put the ruler on the edge of the posterboard and draw a line along the other edge. Then move the ruler down to the line. Groove along the other edge. Do this on all four sides.

Put tape over the corners of the boxes to make them nice and neat.

Bright basket

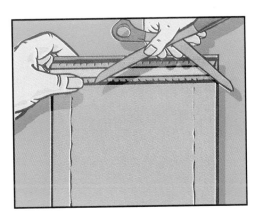

4. Fold up the posterboard into a box shape, with the tabs on the inside, as shown. Tape the tabs to the side of the box, or you can staple or glue them.

5. To make the box lid, make another box. But put the ruler just over the edge of the posterboard when you groove it so that the lid is a little bigger.

To make a deep, square basket, fold the posterboard into a box shape, keeping the sides slanted. Glue the sides together and trim the corners. Glue on a handle.

7

PAPER JEWELS

These paper beads are very easy to make and look like exotic jewelry. Thread them onto colored string to make necklaces or onto thin elastic to make bracelets. Long, thin beads, or two or three small, fat ones, look good as earrings. Try making the beads with the advertisements cut out of magazines or the Sunday comics.

Thread plastic or wooden beads onto your necklace.

Thread different-sized paper beads together.

Things you need

Sheets of colorful or
  patterned paper
Sheets of plain colored paper
Pieces of colored string (about
  2 ft. long)
Thin elastic
Earring fixings (from bead
  or craft shops)
Scissors and glue
Beads

Striped bead necklace

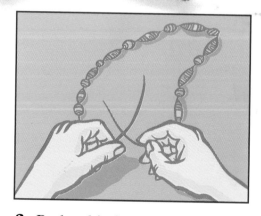

1. Cut out long strips of striped paper that are wide at one end and narrow at the other. Starting at the wide end, roll up a strip with your fingers. Leave a small hole in the middle.

2. When you reach the end of the strip, dab a little glue on the end and press it down gently. Do not squash the bead. Make lots of beads in different-colored stripes and different sizes.

3. Push a big bead onto some string or thin elastic. Put smaller beads on each side. Then thread more beads until you have made a necklace. Leave enough string at each end to tie a bow.

HANDY HINTS

Instead of rolling up the beads with your fingers, try rolling them around a thin knitting needle, a pencil, or a thin stick.

If you want to make a very fat bead, glue two strips of paper together before you roll them up. You can also use thick paper, such as leftover pieces of patterned or plain wallpaper.

To make your jewels, use paper that is colored on both sides or glue two different-colored strips together, back to back.

Easy earrings

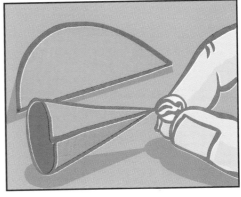

1. Cut out a small circle of colored paper. Cut it in half. Roll each half into a long, thin cone. Glue down the ends. Make a hole through the thin end and attach an earring fixing.

Make a necklace out of different-colored beads.

Make a bracelet with long strips of shiny wrapping paper.

Folded bracelet

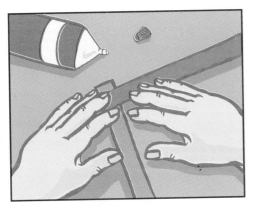

1. Cut two strips of colored paper, each about ¾ in. wide and 2 ft. long. Dab glue on the end of one strip and put the other strip at a right angle to it, as shown. Press it down on the glue.

2. Fold the underneath strip over and press it down. Now fold the other strip over and press it down. Fold over the strips until you reach the ends. Glue the ends together.

Glue two small cones together to make colorful earrings.

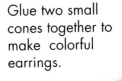

PERKY PAPER DOLLS

You can make a chain of paper dolls long enough to go around a room for party decorations, or short enough to wrap around boxes and lampshades. If you use plain paper, you can color them with paints or crayons. Colored or patterned paper also makes pretty paper dolls.

Things you need

Long strips of plain or
  patterned paper
Pencil, paints,
  or crayons
Glue and tape
Scissors
Lacy paper

To decorate a lampshade, cut out and glue on two shapes together so they bend around the curve.

Cover a plain box with little paper decorations to make it look special.

Singing girls

1. Cut out a long strip of plain paper, about 4 in. wide. Fold it up, backward and forward, like an accordion. Make each fold about 4 in. wide.

2. Draw the shape of a little girl wearing a dress on the top piece of paper, like this. Make sure the shape reaches to each side of the paper at the folds.

3. Hold the folded strip of paper firmly and cut out the little girl shape. Leave a small uncut piece where the shape meets at the folds on each side.

A band of singing girls

Tape different-colored strips of paper together to make these flowers.

Black cat chain

4. To cut out the singing mouths in the girls' faces, fold the paper over sideways down the middle of the face, as shown. Carefully cut out a tiny hole.

5. Make collars out of lacy paper and glue them around the girls' necks. Cut out different-colored paper belts and aprons and glue them onto the dresses, as shown.

6. Cut out two tiny paper eyes for each girl and glue them on their faces. Glue the ends of the strips together to make a long chain to hang up in a room.

11

FANTASTIC FLOWERS

Paper flowers look bright and cheerful in big bunches tied with a bow, or arranged in a vase or small basket. Try using different-colored crepe paper to make the petals for different kinds of flowers. You can make them in all sorts of shapes and sizes.

Things you need

Crepe paper in different
  colors
Stiff paper for leaves
Thin garden wire
  or florist's wire
Paper towels
Scissors, tape, and glue

Make small paper centers for these daffodils. Tape on yellow or white petals and green leaves.

Color the flower centers with paint or felt-tip pens.

12

Use a big bright button as a flower center.

Perfect petals

1. Screw up a little piece of paper towel into a ball. Cover it with another piece. Then tape it to one end of a strip of wire, about 10 in. long.

2. Cut a long strip of crepe paper, about 2½ in. wide. Fold it into squares. Cut out petal shapes. You will need at least five petals for each flower.

3. Stick a small piece of tape on the bottom of a petal. Tape the petal onto the wire, close to the paper ball. Tape on more petals, overlapping each one.

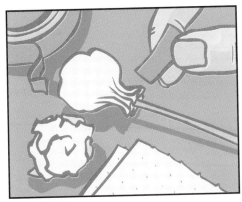

4. Fold a sheet of paper into rectangles. Cut out these leaf shapes. Fold each leaf in half. Crease them down the middle.

5. Cut a long thin strip of crepe paper. Tape one end under the flower. Wind the strip tightly around the wire, to the bottom. Tape down the end.

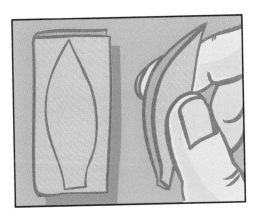

6. Dab glue on the end of a leaf and stick it under the flower. Glue on two more leaves. Then glue leaves down the stem of the flower, as shown.

13

BRIGHT BLOOMS

Here are more paper flowers that are quick and easy to make. You can use them to decorate all sorts of things, such as tables, presents, and branches or twigs. Make them any size you like, from tiny ones that look like flower buds to much bigger ones like these prize carnations.

Things you need

Crepe paper
Stiff paper for leaves
Tape, glue, and scissors

To make a wreath, draw and cut a big ring out of some stiff paper. Glue flowers and leaves around the ring.

Stick colorful flowers on a present.

14

Colorful carnations

1. Cut a strip, about 3 in. wide, off the top of a folded packet of crepe paper, as shown. Unfold the long strip of paper and flatten it out.

2. Cut a rectangle of stiff paper, 6 in. wide and 10 in. long. Roll it up into a thin tube and glue down the edge. This is the flower stem.

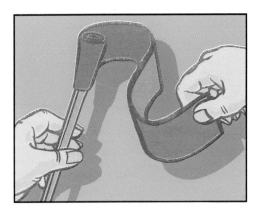

3. Dab glue on one end of the stem. Press the end of the crepe-paper strip onto the glue. Wind the crepe strip around and around the stem.

4. Glue down the end of the strip. Put the end of the scissors into the middle of the crepe paper and cut thin strips all the way around, as shown.

5. Pull the strips outward and bend them down a little to look like the petals of a flower. If the flower stem shows at the center, cut it into thin strips.

6. Fold a piece of stiff paper in half. Cut out two leaf shapes. Fold the two leaves in half. Then stick them onto the top of the stem with tape or glue.

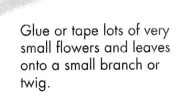

Glue or tape lots of very small flowers and leaves onto a small branch or twig.

HANDY HINTS

To make the flower stems, you can wrap the paper around a thin knitting needle.

Make some carnations with short stems and arrange them in a basket to use as a pretty table decoration.

15

HIGH FLIERS

Surprise your family and friends by making a bird, a beautiful butterfly, or a black bat fly across a room. You can make it fly very fast or flutter slowly. Use colored paper or white paper that you can paint with bright watercolor or poster paints.

Things you need

Stiff white or
  colored paper
Small curtain ring
Very thin nylon string or
  fishing line
Tape and glue
Scissors
Watercolor or
  poster paints
Pencil

Use different-colored papers to make a bird.

Beautiful butterfly

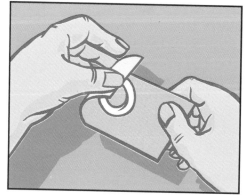

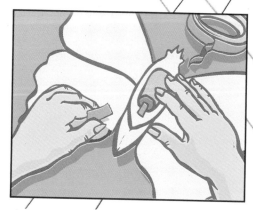

1. Fold a sheet of paper in half. Draw a butterfly's wing on it, and half a butterfly's body on the fold of the paper, as shown. Cut the shape out. Unfold the paper butterfly and flatten it out.

2. Cut out a strip of paper, about 2 in. wide. Roll it around the curtain ring and glue the end down. Make sure the ring is standing upright in the tube of paper, as shown.

3. Push a piece of tape through the paper tube. Press the ends onto the butterfly's body, as shown. Tape on more pieces until the tube is securely attached to the body.

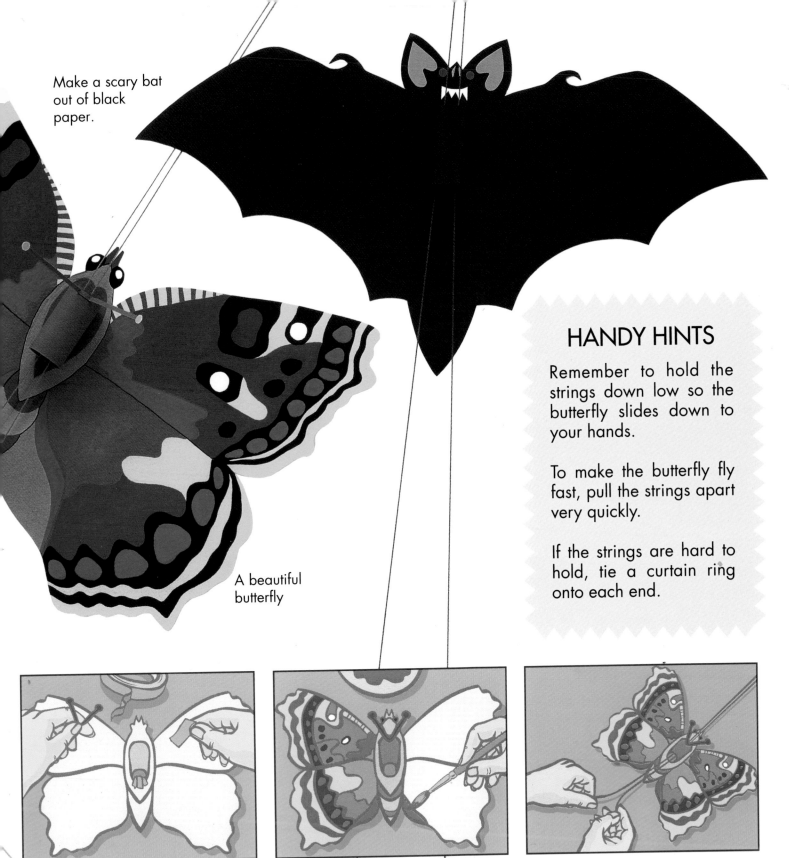

Make a scary bat out of black paper.

A beautiful butterfly

HANDY HINTS

Remember to hold the strings down low so the butterfly slides down to your hands.

To make the butterfly fly fast, pull the strings apart very quickly.

If the strings are hard to hold, tie a curtain ring onto each end.

4. Cut out six thin strips of paper and glue them onto the underneath of the butterfly to make the legs. Glue two thin strips on top of the paper tube to make its antennae.

5. Paint the butterfly with bright colors and patterns. When the paint on one side is dry, turn it over and paint the other side. Hang it up in a safe place and let it dry.

6. Cut a piece of nylon string, about 15 ft. long. Push the ends through the butterfly's body. Loop the string over a hook on the wall or door. Pull the ends of the string apart to make it fly.

17

FRILLY FOREST

This is a tree you can make any size you like. You could make a big one to put on a table as a centerpiece, or a row of little ones for your room. You could also make lots of different-colored trees. Try decorating them with stars cut out of silver or gold paper.

Use gold and red paper to make shiny fir trees for Christmas decorations.

Things you need

Large sheet of thin cardboard or
   thick paper about 19 in. long
   and 9½ in. wide
Cardboard tube from a roll
   of paper towels or foil
Crepe paper
Two pencils and string
Scissors and glue

Use the tubes from toilet paper rolls to make the trunks of small trees.

Use different colors to make a bright tree.

Fringed fir tree

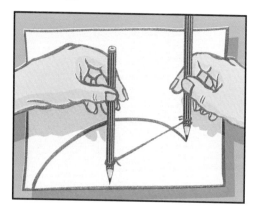

1. Tie the ends of the string to the two pencils. Put one pencil down on the edge of the paper. Draw a half-circle with the other.

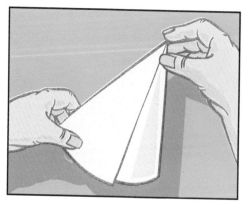

2. Cut out the half-circle of paper and roll it around. Glue the two straight edges together to make a cone, as shown.

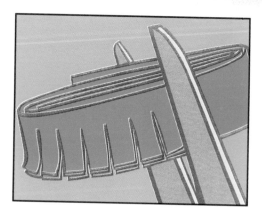

3. Cut long strips of crepe paper, about 2 in. wide. Fold each strip and make cuts along one edge, as shown.

18

Cover a tree with gold, red, or silver stars and lots of candles.

HANDY HINTS

When drawing circles or half-circles with string and two pencils, shorten or lengthen the string so it is half the length of the cardboard.

Cover the cardboard tube with brown paper or paint it brown to make it look like a tree trunk.

To make small trees, use a plate to draw half circles on the cardboard.

You can use almost any kind of paper to make these fir trees. Wrapping paper, shiny paper, and newspaper all make good trees.

Glue small trees in rows on a piece of cardboard.

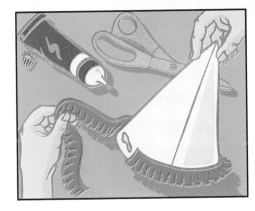

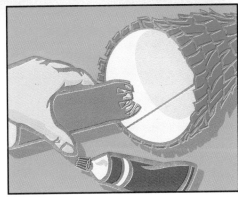

4. Glue a strip of crepe paper loosely around the bottom of the paper cone. Cut off the paper and glue down the end.

5. Glue more strips of crepe paper around the cone. Make sure each new strip just overlaps the one below it.

6. Make little cuts in one end of the cardboard roll. Press them inward. Cover them with glue and press them up into the cone.

POP-UP CARDS

Instead of buying cards to give your friends, why not make your own special cards? These pop-up cards are fun to make and are always a surprise when you open them. Try cutting out different shapes at the top of the cards to make monsters, ghosts, funny faces, or animals.

Things you need

Construction paper in
  different colors
Thin cardboard
Scissors and glue
Paints and felt-tip pens
Pencil

Paint and cut out a birthday cake. Fold it in half and put it inside your card.

Make a flower pop-up to give your mom on Mother's Day.

Slithery snake pop-up card

Witchy pop-up card

20

Witchy pop-up card

1. Fold a sheet of paper, 8 in. long and 4 in. wide, in half. Fold over the top corner, as shown. Fold it back and forth to make a crease.

2. Open the paper. Fold it in half, sideways, so that the bottom edge lines up with the top edge, as shown. Close the card, pulling out the fold.

3. Inside the card draw a witch shape where it pops out. Cut out the shape. Paint the card and write a message on the outside and on the inside.

Slithery snake card

1. Fold a piece of thin cardboard, about 9½ in. by 4¾ in., in half. Press the fold down firmly. Cut out a piece of paper the same size as the folded card.

2. Cut off the corners of the piece of paper to make a neat circle. Cut the paper around and around from one edge toward the middle, as shown.

3. Paint the coil to look like a long, slithery snake. Cut out a forked tongue and glue it on. Glue the tail to the top of the card, as shown.

HANDY HINTS

When you fold the cardboard or paper, put the edges together so they meet exactly. Then the cards will look very neat.

To make cards that really pop out, fold them very carefully and press the folds down very hard to make good creases.

Decide what you want your card to look like before you start. You can get some very good ideas from picture books and magazines.

So that you don't make any mistakes, first draw the picture on a piece of paper and then copy it onto the cardboard or paper.

CRAZY CARDS

These crazy cards make good birthday and Christmas cards or party invitations. You can make them any size you like. If you have very big sheets of paper or cardboard, try making giant cards that will really surprise your friends.

Things you need

Thick paper or posterboard,
  both white and colored
Scissors and glue
Paints and felt-tip pens

HANDY HINTS

Use bright wrapping paper to make colorful strips for the busy cards.

Make a moving card that opens upward and pulls downward to open the door.

Open up a moving card so you can draw or paint a picture behind the door. Or cut out a picture from a magazine and glue it behind the door.

PULL

Be my valentine card

Busy cards

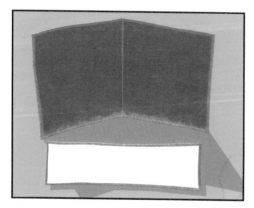

1. Cut a piece of posterboard the size you want your card to be and fold it in half. Cut a wide strip of paper slightly smaller than the card when it is opened up, as shown.

2. Fold the strip of paper in four equal parts. Draw a picture, like a snowman, on the front. Cut it out, leaving a link at each side. Open the paper. Paint the snowmen. Glue each end to the edge of the card.

3. Cut two narrow strips of paper. Fold them both in four equal parts. Draw a pattern on them and cut them out, leaving the links at each side. Glue the strips onto the top and bottom of the card.

22

Mother's Day card

Busy birthday card

Crazy Christmas card

Get-well card

PULL

Moving cards

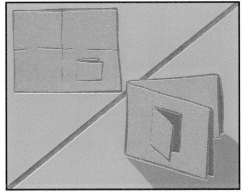

1. Fold a sheet of thick paper in half. Unfold it and fold it in half the other way. Open it out and cut a door in the bottom right square, as shown. Fold up the card.

2. Cut a strip of paper, almost as long as the open card. Cut two slits on the inside of the card, each a little longer than the width of the strip. Push the strip through the slits, as shown.

3. Glue the end of the strip to the edge of the door. Decorate the card. Write a message or draw a picture behind the door. Close the door. Write "PULL" on the end of the paper strip.

23

CLEVER COLLAGES

Collages are pictures and decorations made of cut-out or torn-out pictures and different kinds of paper. They make very good posters and calendars or party invitations. You can also use them to decorate cards and boxes, and to make pictures for presents. Photographs and advertisements from color magazines, vacation brochures, and some mail-order catalogs are all good for collages.

HANDY HINTS

If you want paper with a jagged edge, tear it instead of using scissors.

When you are making a poster for a sale, party, or other event, remember to write in the place where it will be, the day, the date, and the time.

If you want to cut out very small pictures, use small scissors to get nice neat edges.

Things you need

Large sheets of paper or
   posterboard
Different kinds of
   colored paper,
   photographs, and
   advertisements
Glue and scissors
Pencil and ruler
Felt-tip pens and paints
Printed calendar
Ribbon

Silly picture

Calendar collage

1. Using a pencil and ruler, draw lines across a sheet of poster-board from the corners, as shown. Glue a calendar where the lines cross. This is the middle of the paper.

2. Tear strips of colored paper and glue them to the top and bottom of the posterboard. Cut out pictures; glue them around the calendar to make a scene, as shown. Let the glue dry.

3. Cut a piece of ribbon 2 in. long. Fold it in half, in a **V** shape. Glue the ends to the top of the back of the calendar to make a loop. When the glue is dry, hang up the calendar by the loop.

Spooky poster

Silly pictures

1. Draw lines with a pencil and ruler on a big sheet of paper. Write in the words you want on your spooky poster, spacing out the letters neatly. Fill them in with felt-tip pens or paint.

2. Cut out and glue colored pictures around the words. Choose spooky pictures to go with the theme. Glue the poster onto a piece of posterboard and tear around the edges.

Cut out a big photograph or advertisement and glue on lots of little pictures. Use photos of your family or of friends or animals, or just silly things to make a funny picture.

Collage calendar

Use different kinds of paper with odd textures, such as newspaper, tissue paper, or corrugated paper.

Spooky poster

HALLOWEEN PARTY AT BRAD'S HOUSE SAT. OCTOBER 31st, 6:00pm

PAPER WILDLIFE PARK

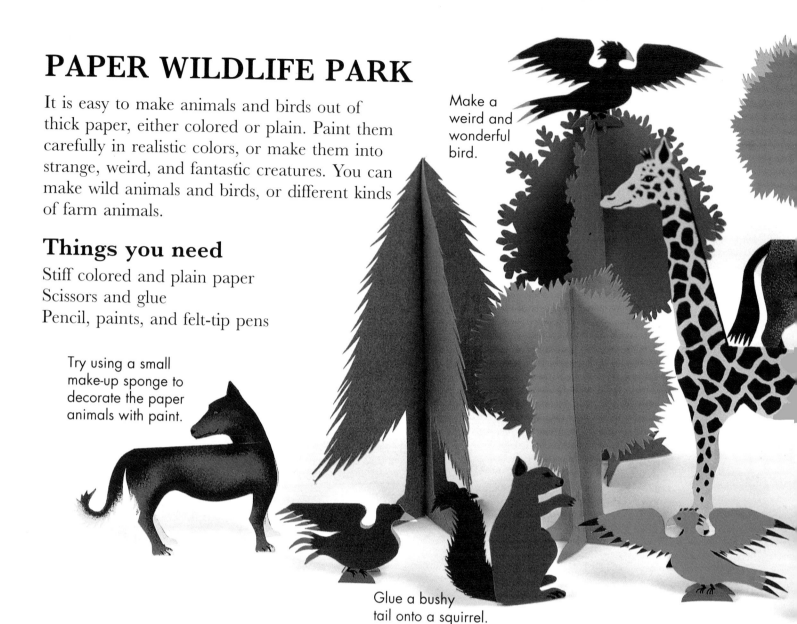

It is easy to make animals and birds out of thick paper, either colored or plain. Paint them carefully in realistic colors, or make them into strange, weird, and fantastic creatures. You can make wild animals and birds, or different kinds of farm animals.

Things you need

Stiff colored and plain paper
Scissors and glue
Pencil, paints, and felt-tip pens

Try using a small make-up sponge to decorate the paper animals with paint.

Make a weird and wonderful bird.

Glue a bushy tail onto a squirrel.

Tiger

Draw a tiger shape, as you did the giraffe's. Cut it out and paint it. Glue the sides of its head together, and then glue the tail.

Giraffe

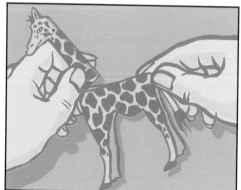

Draw a giraffe's body on a piece of folded paper, with its back on the fold. Cut it out. Draw neck and head on stiff paper. Cut it out. Cut a slit in the backbone. Glue neck into it. Paint giraffe.

Elephant

Draw and cut out an elephant with its backbone along the fold of the paper. Glue on its trunk and then its tail. Cut two big ears. Glue them to the head. Paint the elephant.

Make trees in different shapes and sizes.

Give the lion a fringed paper mane.

HANDY HINTS

If you want to make big animals, you need thin cardboard, rather than stiff paper, to make them stand up properly.

An animal with a long neck falls over unless you cut out the legs well forward. You should also give it big feet to balance it.

Always remember to draw each animal with its backbone along the fold in the paper. Otherwise it will fall apart.

Duck

Paper trees

Draw and cut out a duck's body as you did the giraffe's. Draw and cut out a head and neck. Glue the neck into a slit on the duck's backbone. Glue two wings to the body. Paint the duck.

1. Fold a sheet of stiff paper in half. With a pencil, draw the shape of a tree with a thick trunk, about 2 in. high. Cut out the tree shape.

2. Cut a slit up the trunk of one tree. Cut the other tree from the top to the trunk. Slot the two together, as shown. Glue them together along the slits.

PAPER PEOPLE

These two pages show you how to make paper people in lots of different shapes and sizes. Try making a family of paper people, a clown, a strange magician, an angel, or a nasty monster. You can glue on paper eyes and mouths, paper hair, horns, big ears, some scary paper teeth, a beard, or a curly mustache.

Things you need

Cardboard tubes from
  toilet paper, paper towel,
  or tinfoil rolls
Plain and colored paper
Paper towels
Cardboard
Glue, scissors, tape, and a
  pencil
Paints or felt-tip pens
Newspaper

Give the magician an exotic hat, cape, and beard.

Paint the clown's clothes or decorate them with paper shapes.

Clown

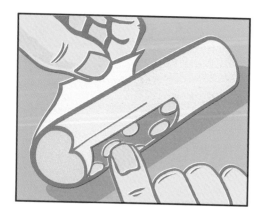

1. To make the clown's legs, make a groove with scissors halfway down a long cardboard tube. Glue colored paper around the legs. Glue a different color around the top half of the tube.

2. For the arms, cut out two pieces of stiff paper, 5 in. long and 2 in. wide. Roll each piece into a tube and glue the edges. Cut one end of each arm at an angle and glue it onto the tube.

3. To make the clown's head, scrunch up some newspaper into a ball. Then wrap a paper towel around it. Push the neck into the top of the tube and tape it in place. Glue on cardboard feet.

28

Dumpies

1. For the body and head, wrap two pieces of paper around a short cardboard tube. Glue down the edges. Cut out cardboard feet and glue them onto the end of the tube, as shown.

2. Fold a piece of stiff paper in half. Draw an arm and hand shape and cut it out. Glue an arm to each side of the body. For hair, make lots of cuts in a strip of thin paper. Glue it on.

3. To make a hat, cut out a small circle of paper. Make one cut to the middle of the circle, as shown. Overlap the edges and glue them down. Glue the hat on the top of the Dumpy.

Decorate the Dumpies' clothes with paper shapes.

You can use gift-wrapping ribbon to make an angel with shiny paper hair.

HANDY HINTS

If you don't have any cardboard tubes, roll a piece of thin cardboard into a tube and glue or tape down the edge.

To make a tall cone, roll up a sheet of paper. Make one end pointed and the other end wide. Glue down the edge of the paper. Cut off the top and bottom to make neat edges.

HANDSOME HATS

You can make all sorts of different paper hats to wear at parties or just for fun. Ask your friends to come to a fancy hat party wearing their own crazy paper hats. The person with the best hat can win a prize.

Things you need

Posterboard or large sheets of
   construction paper in different
   colors
Gold and silver paper
Scissors, pencil, and glue
Paints or felt-tip pens
Small colorful candies

For a clown's hat, cut out different-colored paper dots and stick them onto a tall cone hat. Stick shapes around the bottom.

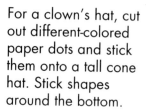

Use a black felt-tip pen to decorate the cotton wool on your crown. Then it will look like real ermine.

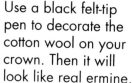

To make a cap, cut out a bill of stiff paper and glue it onto a round hat that does not have a brim.

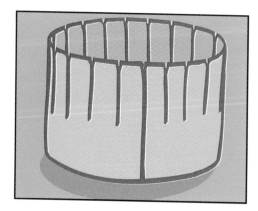

Round hat

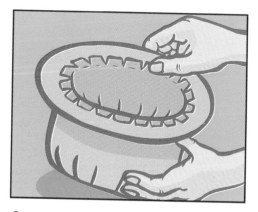

1. Cut a strip of paper, about 10 in. wide and long enough to go around your head. Cut slits, about halfway down, all along the strip. Glue the ends of the strip together, as shown.

2. Bend over a strip on each side and glue the ends together in the middle. Glue two strips from the two other sides in the middle. Glue together, one pair at a time, all the other strips.

3. Put the hat down on a sheet of paper. Carefully draw around it. Cut out the circle and a wider one around it for the brim. Cut small slits around the bottom of the hat. Glue them to the brim.

30

Make a witch's hat out of black paper. Glue on spooky shapes.

Roll strips of tinfoil into little wheels to glue onto a crown.

Crazy crown

Cone hat

1. Cut a strip of gold paper, about 6 in. wide and long enough to go around your head. Fold it in three but do not crease the edges. Draw a crown shape, as shown, and then cut it out.

2. Unfold the paper and glue the ends together. Cut out jewel shapes from shiny paper. Glue them around the crown. You can also glue on small colorful candies as jewels.

Cut a piece of paper, 1 ft. wide and long enough to go around your head. Roll it into a cone, and glue the edges. Cut off the extra paper. Paint the hat, or cut out shapes and glue them onto it.

MARVELOUS MASKS

Masks are fun to wear at costume parties or on special occasions like Halloween. Make some for your friends, or choose a theme such as animal, alien, or spooky masks and ask them to make their own. Once you have made the base, you can add things like hair, eyelashes, feathers, or whiskers. You can make small eye masks or whole face masks.

Things you need

Sheets of thick plain and
  colored paper
Colored paper to decorate
  your mask
Thin rolled elastic
Big needle
Glue, scissors, and tape
Pencil

Make a space mask out of silver paper. Glue on tinfoil and other space-age objects.

Draw and paint a car, like this Beetle, on stiff cardboard. Cut out the middle of the wheels as eye holes. Fasten on elastic for the headband.

Crafty cat mask

1. Draw this mask shape on a sheet of thick paper. Make it about 2¼ in. deep and 4¾ in. wide. Cut it out. Cut out two eye holes in the middle of the mask, about 1 in. apart.

2. Cut two small ear shapes out of pink paper. Glue one to the inside of each ear. Cut out whiskers and a nose. Then glue them onto the mask.

3. Add more decorations. Then wrap a length of elastic around your head and cut it to fit. Thread it through a needle and through the mask, as shown. Knot each end at the holes in the mask.

To be sure that a mask will fit you, hold a sheet of paper against your face and mark where your eyes are with a pencil. Then carefully cut out the eye holes.

Instead of decorating your mask with paper shapes, you can paint it with poster paints. The paint may make the paper a little bit floppy. Let it dry and it will stiffen again.

To make a really jazzy mask, glue on sequins feathers, sparkles, beads, or buttons.

Crazy face mask

1. Draw a face, about 8 in. high and 4¾ in. wide, on some paper. Draw two eyes, 1 in. apart, a nose, and a mouth. Cut out the face. Cut out the eye holes and a flap for the nose.

2. Fold a second sheet of paper. Cut out two ears. Tape one to each side of the face. Cut out decorations, such as bright paper flowers and dangling earrings, to glue or tape on your mask.

3. To make a really crazy face, glue on paper eyelashes, spiky hair, and red lips. Measure a piece of elastic around your head. Thread it through a needle and knot it onto the mask.

PRETTY PLATES

You can make wonderful plates and bowls in many different shapes using old newspapers, flour, and water. Brightly painted and varnished, they make beautiful decorations and good presents. Instead of painting them, try covering your plates with colorful tissue paper or pictures cut out of magazines.

Things you need

Old newspapers
Flour and water
Bowl for mixing and a tablespoon
Plastic wrap or petroleum jelly
Old plate or bowl
Poster paints and a paintbrush
Scissors and water-based varnish

Painted plate

Tissue-paper plate

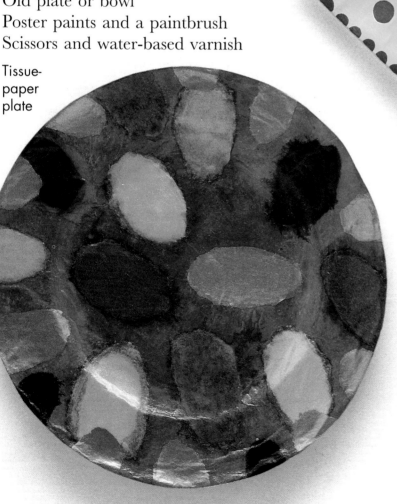

HANDY HINTS

Try using different-shaped plates and bowls. But don't use ones that slope inward at the top or you won't be able to take your paper plate or bowl off when it is finished.

Rest the plate on a small bowl to keep it away from the tabletop so that you can easily glue bits of newspaper around the edge.

Instead of using flour and water, you can use ordinary wallpaper paste.

Painted paper plate

1. To make the paste, put two tablespoons of flour in a bowl and add four or five tablespoons of cold water. Stir it well until it is like thin cream. Add more water if it is too thick.

2. Hold four pages of newspaper together and tear them into strips, about 1 in. wide. Then tear the strips into little squares, about the size of large postage stamps, as shown.

3. Cover a plate with plastic wrap to keep the paper from sticking. Wrap it tightly and smooth down all the folds. Instead of plastic wrap you can cover the plate with petroleum jelly.

4. Brush a layer of flour paste onto the plate. Cover it with a layer of newspaper squares, over-lapping the edges. Brush on more paste. Put on a second layer of newspaper. Let it dry.

5. Repeat step 4 until you have five or six layers. Let the newspaper dry completely. When it is dry, cut around the plate or bowl with scissors to make a nice neat edge.

6. Carefully take off the dried paper from the plate or bowl. Then remove the plastic wrap. Paint the paper plate with poster paints. When it is dry, brush on varnish and let it dry again.

Cover a bowl with pictures cut out of a magazine.

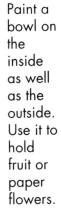

Paint a bowl on the inside as well as the outside. Use it to hold fruit or paper flowers.

35

FANCY LANTERNS

Paper lanterns look good as party decorations or just to decorate your room. You can make them in different colors and paint on extra designs. Glitter paint makes them sparkle. Make them any size you like and hang them up on their own or in a row. Just be sure not to put light bulbs or candles inside of them.

To make them even fancier, paint different patterns on your lanterns.

Things you need

Construction paper in different colors
Very thin colored paper
Big and small plates
Scissors and glue
Pencil
Poster paints, glitter paint, and a paintbrush

A really big lantern looks good hanging from the ceiling.

Fancy lantern

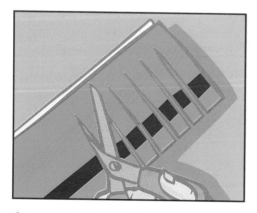

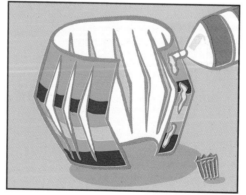

1. Fold a sheet of construction paper in half, lengthwise. Crease it down the middle. Make deep cuts all the way along the folded edge.

2. Unfold the paper. Spread glue along the two short edges, as shown. Bend the paper around and press the edges together until they are firmly glued.

3. Cut a narrow strip of paper for the handle. Glue each end to the top of the lantern, on the inside. Let it dry before you hang up the lantern.

36

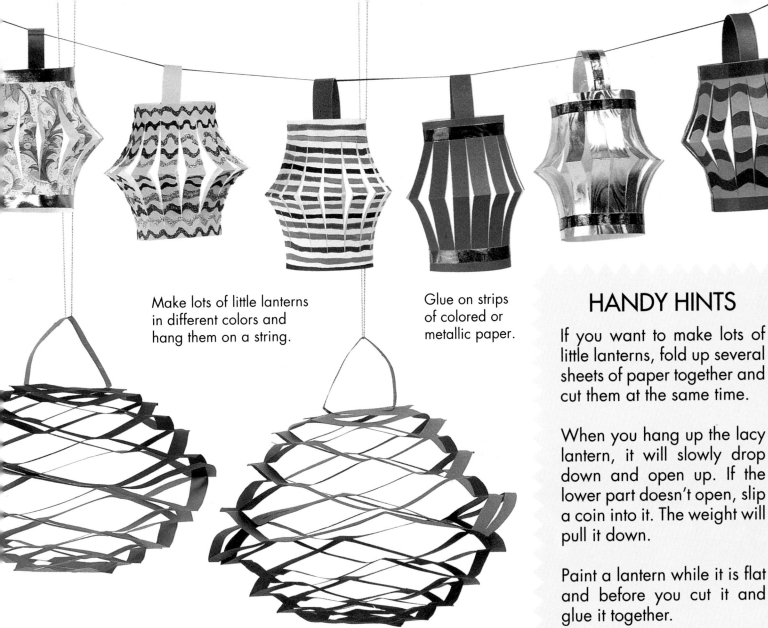

Make lots of little lanterns in different colors and hang them on a string.

Glue on strips of colored or metallic paper.

HANDY HINTS

If you want to make lots of little lanterns, fold up several sheets of paper together and cut them at the same time.

When you hang up the lacy lantern, it will slowly drop down and open up. If the lower part doesn't open, slip a coin into it. The weight will pull it down.

Paint a lantern while it is flat and before you cut it and glue it together.

Lacy lantern

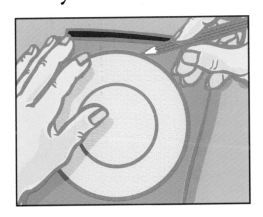

1. Put two sheets of very thin paper on top of each other. Put a plate down on top of them and draw a circle around it. Cut out the circles and pull them apart.

2. Fold one circle in half, then in half again, and again. Make cuts along both edges, as shown. Do the same to the second circle. Open both circles.

3. Carefully glue the two circles together at the edges. Cut out a strip of paper for the handle. Glue the ends to the middle of one circle. Let the glue dry.

DAZZLING DECORATIONS

Use shiny paper in bright colors to make these dazzling decorations. Make little ones to hang on the Christmas tree. Or light up a room with rows of golden angels, silver bells, and sparkling paper chains.

Things you need

Shiny wrapping paper, including
 gold and silver
Thin paper in bright colors
Scissors and glue
Plate and
 cup

Hang chains,
bells, and angels
across a room.

Use two
different
colors to
make the
lacy balls.

Lacy balls

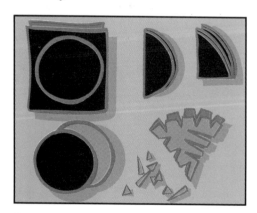

1. Put two sheets of paper on top of each other. Draw a circle around a cup on the paper. Cut it out. Fold each circle of paper in half, in half again, and again. Snip bits out of the sides.

2. Unfold the two circles. Fold each one in half. Tape or glue them together at the folds. Glue on a thin paper handle as shown. Space out the four sides of the lacy ball.

HANDY HINTS

To make chains really quickly, fold up a big sheet of paper so that you can cut out lots of strips at the same time.

To make decorations of different sizes, try using different-sized plates or cups to draw around.

Instead of using thin paper to make the lacy balls, you can use tissue paper.

38

Bright bells

To make a cone, draw around a plate on a piece of paper. Cut out the circle. Cut it in half. Roll half into a cone; glue the edges. Glue on a paper handle and ringer.

Hang the candy cones up on a ribbon.

Golden angel

Make a cone out of shiny gold paper. Draw a wing shape, as shown, on a folded piece of paper. Cut it out. Glue the wings to the cone. Then glue on a head and a thin handle.

Glue paper eyes, a mouth, and a halo on the angel's face.

Candy cone

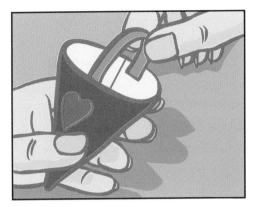

Make a cone and turn it upside down. Cut a thin paper handle and glue it on, as shown. When the glue is dry, fill the cone with little candies, cookies, or very small presents.

Sparkling chains

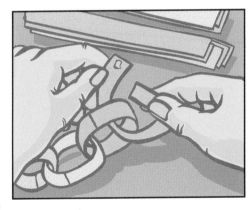

Cut out strips of shiny paper, about 8 in. long and 1 in. wide. Glue the ends of a strip together. Loop a second strip through it and glue the ends. Add more strips to make a long chain.

PERFECT PAPER FRUIT

Paper fruit is easy to make and looks like real fruit! Try making different kinds of fruit, such as apples, bananas, pears, or oranges, any size you like. They look good in a bowl, as a table decoration, or hanging from an indoor plant or tree.

Things you need

Old newspaper
Plain paper
White flour and a
  tablespoon
Bowl for mixing
Plastic wrap
Scissors and glue
Poster paints and
  a paintbrush
Pencil

Round orange

Red and green apples

A perfect pear

Paper apple

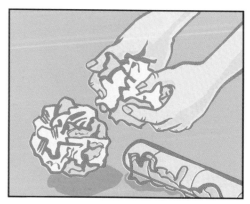

1. Put one tablespoon of flour in the bowl. Add three or four tablespoons of water. Stir it well until it is like thin cream without any lumps in it.

2. Tear a sheet of newspaper into long strips, about 1 in. wide. Tear the long strips into small squares, about the size of large postage stamps.

3. Scrunch up two sheets of newspaper very tightly into a ball or the shape you want the fruit to be. Put plastic wrap around it to help it keep its shape.

40

Purple plums

Lovely lemon

Big banana

HANDY HINTS

To make shiny, beautiful fruit that lasts longer, brush on a layer of water-based varnish.

Smooth down the newspaper squares with your fingers to get a smooth, round shape.

Instead of using plastic wrap, you can wrap masking tape around the fruit.

To make your fruit look like real fruit, dab on the paint with a tiny sponge.

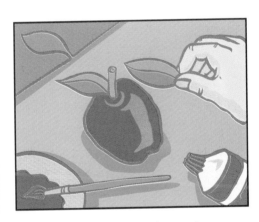

4. Brush paste over the fruit shape. Cover it with newspaper squares, making sure they all overlap. Brush on more paste. Put on a second layer of paper.

5. For a stalk, cut out a small square of white paper. Roll it up. Glue down the edge. Make a hole with a pencil in the top of the fruit and stick the stalk in.

6. Let the fruit dry for at least one day. Then paint it all over with a thick layer of paint. Cut out paper leaves and glue them to the stalk.

MADCAP MOBILES

Make this spooky mobile, or design your own special mobile to hang up from a lampshade or any high place in a room. Mobiles make good presents to give to young children and babies to decorate their bedrooms. They love to watch them slowly twist and turn as they lie in bed.

Things you need

Colored drinking straws
Construction paper in different colors
Glow-in-the-dark paper or pens
Strong thread and a big needle
Tape, pencil, and scissors
Paints or felt-tip pens

HANDY HINTS

If a mobile does not hang level, slide the thread along a straw a little. Move it until the straws hang right.

Make a zany space mobile.

Spooky mobile

1. Put the ends of two straws together. They must be exactly the same size and length. Wind tape around them to make a long straw. Make two more long straws in the same way.

2. Draw seven spooky shapes, such as a bat, ghost, skeleton, pumpkin, or wicked witch, on construction paper. They should all be about the same size. Cut them out.

3. Put the middles of the three long straws across each other. Tape them together, one at a time, as shown. Make sure that the space between each one is the same.

42

Tie on more
straws, threads,
and shapes to
make a very
busy mobile.

Fishy
mobile

4. Cut eight pieces of thread,
each about 20 in. long. Thread
one through the needle. Push the
needle through the middle of the
straws, as shown. Tie the thread
in a knot around them.

5. Paint or color the seven
spooky shapes. Give them long,
sharp teeth, scary faces, or black
clothes. Glue on bits of glow-in-
the-dark paper for the eyes and
mouths. Let them dry.

6. Stick one end of a thread
through the top of each monster.
Stick the other ends through the
straws and one from the center.
Knot the thread ends. Hang the
mobile by the middle thread.

FABULOUS FOLDERS

Folders are very useful for keeping letters, secret papers, and all kinds of odds and ends in. They also make very good presents for your friends and family. You can decorate them with drawings or paintings, or glue on cut-out pictures or patterns made from colored paper.

Things you need

Plain or colored posterboard
Glue, scissors, and
  paper-fasteners
Ribbon and string
Pencil and ruler
Large coin

Decorate your folder with pictures and patterns cut out of magazines or made from colored paper.

Fancy folder

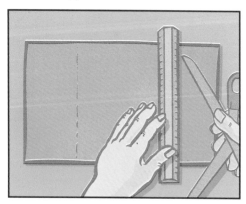

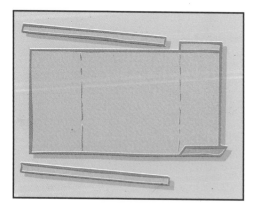

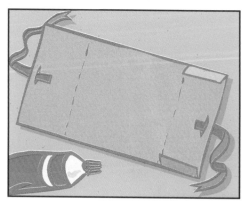

1. Cut out a piece of posterboard, about 20 in. long and 13 in. wide. Measure 6 in. from one edge and make a groove with scissors, as shown. Measure 5 in. from the other edge. Make another groove there.

2. Measure ½ in. along the top and bottom edges. Draw two lines. Cut off the strips to the second groove. Fold the posterboard along the lines. Fold over the strips and press along the creases, as shown.

3. Cut a small slit at each end of the posterboard, as shown. Cut two pieces of ribbon, 12 in. long. Push the end of one ribbon through a slit. Glue down the end. Then glue on the other ribbon.

44

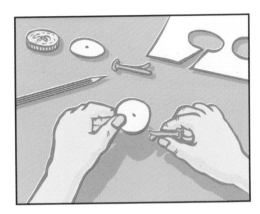

Folder with fasteners

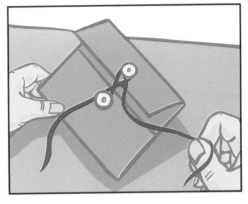

1. Draw two circles around a large coin on posterboard. Cut out the circles. Make a small hole in the middle of each circle with scissors. Push a paper-fastener into each hole.

2. Push each fastener into the folder near the edges and press down the prongs. Wind some string, 8 in. long, around one fastener, under one circle, and then around the other.

Paint on a friend's name and give the folder away as a present.

HANDY HINTS

You can make folders of any size. All you need is a piece of posterboard about twice as long as it is wide.

When you fold up a folder along the grooves, press the closed scissors along the lines to make a good crease.

4. Fold up the strips on the top and bottom of the posterboard. Fold up the right-hand side of the posterboard and glue down the strips. Close the folder and tie the ribbons in a neat bow.

Give everyone in your secret club his or her own special folder.

CLEVER CARDBOARD CLOCKS

You can use all sorts of cardboard boxes to make interesting clocks. This is a simple one but you can invent your own shapes. Use one to teach a small child how to tell time. Or make a clock each for your mom and dad. They can use them to tell each other what time they are going out or when they will be home.

To make an elegant clock, glue on pieces of metallic paper.

Things you need

Small cardboard boxes
Plain and colored paper
Thin cardboard
Pins or very small
  nails
Glue, scissors, and tape
Poster paints or
  felt-tip pens
Cup or small jar

Glue on funny hands and feet.

Clever clock

1. Shut the lid of a small, sturdy, rectangular cardboard box. Tape down the lid and the open sides with strong tape. Then neatly snip off any extra pieces of tape, as shown.

2. Cut a piece of thin cardboard the same width as the sides of the box and twice as long as the top. Fold the cardboard in half and tape it to the sides of the box to make a roof, as shown.

3. Cut two small pieces of thin cardboard and tape them to the front and back of the box. Cut off the extra cardboard at the top, as shown. Tape down the edges of the roof.

Make different-shaped hands like these fishy ones.

Paint Roman numerals on a castle clock.

Paint bright numbers all over your clock.

4. Wrap the box in a sheet of paper. Glue it on. Cut off the extra pieces around the roof, as shown. Glue down the paper on the roof.

5. Draw a circle around a cup or small jar on a sheet of paper. Cut it out. Write the numbers 1 to 12 neatly around the circle to look like a clock. Glue the circle to the front of the box.

6. For the hands, draw one big and one small arrow on some thin cardboard. Cut them out. Push a pin through both hands. Then push the pin through the middle of the clock face.

47

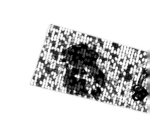